Classics for Beginning Readers ™

Reader's Digest Young Families

D1712241

The Velveteen Rabbit

Designers: Elaine Lopez and Wendy Boccuzzi
Editor: Suzanne G. Beason
Associate Editorial Director: Pamela Pia

Adapted text copyright © 2003 Reader's Digest Young Families, Inc.
Based on the original story written by Margery Williams in 1922.
Adapted by Sarah Albee.
Illustrations by Jeff Fisher © 2003 Reader's Digest Young Families, Inc.

Printed in China.

Classics for Beginning Readers™

Reader's Digest Young Families

The Velveteen Rabbit

Based on the story written in 1922
by
Margery Williams

Retold by Sarah Albee

Illustrations by
Jeff Fisher

$\mathcal{O}$nce there was a Velveteen Rabbit. He was fat and bunchy. He had brown and white spots, real thread whiskers, and pink satin ears. He sat in the top of the Boy's stocking on Christmas morning.

The Boy loved the Rabbit. But there were many other toys for the Boy, too. In the excitement of looking at the new presents, the Velveteen Rabbit was forgotten. For a long time, the Rabbit lived in the toy chest.

The other toys in the nursery felt that they were better than the Rabbit. The mechanical toys were full of modern ideas. There was a model boat that liked to use big words, and a lion with legs that could bend. The Rabbit felt unimportant compared to the other toys, especially since he was only stuffed with sawdust.

The one toy that was kind to the little Rabbit was the Skin Horse. He had lived in the nursery longer than any other toy. He had belonged to the Boy's uncle.

The Skin Horse was very old, and most of his tail had been pulled out to make necklaces, and some of his coat had been rubbed away. But he was very wise. He understood all about nursery magic and often talked about being Real.

"What is REAL?" asked the Velveteen Rabbit. "Does it mean having things that buzz inside you and a stick-out handle?"

"Real is not how you are made," replied the Skin Horse. "A toy becomes Real only when a child really loves it. Fancy toys that can be broken easily never become Real because they break too quickly. It takes a long, long time to become Real. Often, by the time you become Real, most of your hair is rubbed away and you look very shabby."

"Are you Real?" asked the Rabbit.

"Yes," replied the Skin Horse. "The Boy's Uncle made me Real, many years ago. Being Real lasts forever." The Rabbit sighed. He wished the magic would happen to him so that he could become Real as well.

There was a person called Nana who ruled the nursery. She often came to tidy up and put toys away.

One evening at bedtime, the Boy asked for his china dog. Nana was in a hurry and couldn't find the dog. So she grabbed the Rabbit instead.

"Here," she said to the Boy. "Take your old Bunny instead." The Velveteen Rabbit slept with the Boy that night, and for many nights after.

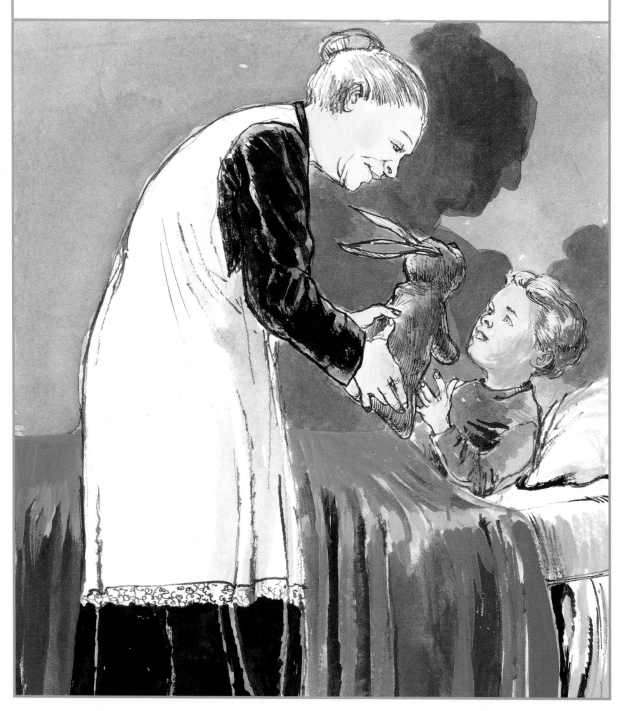

At first the Rabbit did not like being in the Boy's bed. The Boy hugged him very tight, and sometimes rolled over on him. But soon he grew to like it. The Boy would talk to him. They would play games together. After the Boy fell asleep, the Rabbit would snuggle close to him all night long.

And so time went on, and the little Rabbit was very happy. He did not notice how shabby his fur was becoming, or how all the pink had rubbed off his nose where the Boy had so often kissed him.

Spring came, and the two played together everywhere. They played in the garden, and had picnics in the grass.

Once, the Rabbit was left out on the lawn after dark. Nana had to go out with a light to find the Rabbit, since the Boy could not sleep without him. When she finally found him, he was wet with dew, and dirty from the garden.

"What a fuss you are making for a toy!" grumbled Nana. She wiped the Rabbit clean with a cloth.

"You mustn't say that," said the Boy, sitting up in bed. "He isn't a toy. He's REAL!"

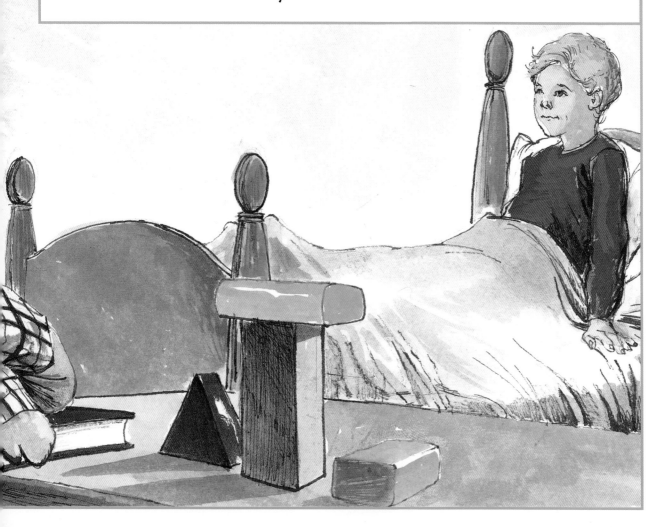

When the little Rabbit heard that he was so happy. He was Real! The Boy himself had said it. That was a wonderful summer. The Boy often took his Velveteen Rabbit to the woods near the house. Before he went off to pick flowers, the Boy always made sure his Rabbit was sitting in a cozy place. One day, the Rabbit saw two strange creatures creep out of the bushes near him.

They were rabbits just like him. But these rabbits looked furry and new. They crept close to him, twitching their noses. The Velveteen Rabbit stared hard at them, trying to see where their seams and wind-up key might be. But he could see nothing.

"Why don't you get up and play with us?" asked one. "Can't you hop on your hind legs like this?" He gave a hop.

"I don't feel like it," said the Velveteen Rabbit. He felt awful, for he had no hind legs at all. The back of him was all one piece, like a pincushion.

But wild rabbits have sharp eyes. "He hasn't got any hind legs!" called one of them, laughing. "And he doesn't smell right! He isn't a rabbit at all! He isn't real!"

"I am Real!" said the little Rabbit. "The Boy said so!" Just then the Boy ran past them, and the two wild rabbits hopped away. For a long time the Velveteen Rabbit lay very still, hoping they would come back. Then the Boy came and carried him home.

Weeks passed, and the little Rabbit grew very shabby. But the Boy loved him just as much. And then, one day, the Boy was ill.

His face grew flushed. His body was so hot it burned the Rabbit when he held him close. Strange people came and went, and a light burned all night. The Velveteen Rabbit lay under the covers without stirring, afraid someone might take him away if they found him. He knew that the Boy needed him.

The Boy was sick for a long time. He was too ill to play, and the little Rabbit found it dull with nothing to do all day. But he waited patiently for the Boy to get better. As the Boy lay half-asleep the Rabbit crept close to the pillow and whispered in his ear. He talked to the Boy about how they would go into the garden and play games together just as they used to, as soon as he became well again.

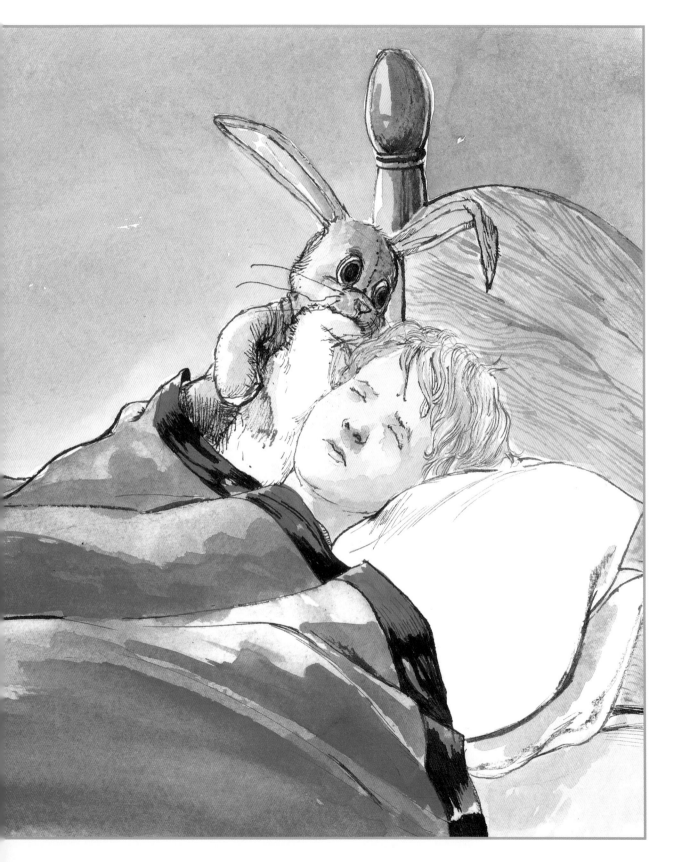

At last the Boy got better. One day they let him get up and dress. They carried him out to the balcony. He was to go to the seaside the next day. The Rabbit was excited to go to the seaside. The Boy had talked about it often.

Then the doctor ordered all the books and toys and bedclothes to be burnt. The room had to be disinfected.

"What about his old Bunny?" asked Nana.

"It is full of scarlet fever germs!" said the doctor. "Get him a new rabbit and burn this one at once."

So the little Rabbit was put into a sack along with the picture books and other toys. The gardener was supposed to make a big bonfire, but he was too busy just at that moment. He decided to take care of it early the next morning.

That night the Boy slept in a new room. He had a new bunny to sleep with. He was so excited to go to the seaside, he didn't think about his new bunny very much.

While the Boy was asleep, the Rabbit was in the backyard, lying in the sack with the toys and picture books. He felt very lonely.

The sack had been left untied, so the little Rabbit peeked out. He shivered a little, for he was used to sleeping in a warm bed. His coat had become so thin from hugging that it didn't protect him from the cold.

Nearby were some raspberry bushes. He and the Boy had played here many times. He thought about those times and felt very sad. He thought of the Skin Horse, whom he would never see again. And then a tear trickled down his shabby velvet nose and fell onto the ground.

Suddenly a flower grew out of the ground, just where the tear had fallen. It had beautiful green leaves and a blossom that looked like a golden cup. The blossom opened and out stepped a fairy.

Her dress was made of pearls and dewdrops. Her face was as beautiful as a flower. She put her arms around the little Rabbit and kissed him on his nose.

"I am the nursery magic Fairy," she said. "I take care of all the playthings that children have loved and make them Real."

"Wasn't I Real before?" asked the Rabbit.

"You were Real to the Boy," she said. "Now you shall be Real to everyone."

The Fairy held the Velveteen Rabbit in her arms and flew with him into the woods. The moon had risen. Wild rabbits danced in the velvet grass.

"I've brought you a new playmate," said the Fairy to the wild rabbits. "He will live with you forever. Run and play, little Rabbit!"

At first the little Rabbit felt shy, because he had no hind legs. But then something tickled his nose, and without thinking about what he was doing, he lifted his back leg to scratch it.

The Velveteen Rabbit had hind legs! His ears twitched by themselves, and his fur was soft and brown. He gave a leap of joy. He had become a Real Rabbit at last. When he turned around to look for the Fairy, she had gone.

Autumn passed, and then Winter did too. In the Spring, when the days were warm and sunny, the Boy went out to play in the woods. One day while he was playing, two rabbits crept out to peek at him. One of them had brown and white spots and an expression in his eyes that seemed strangely familiar to the Boy.

"Why, he looks just like my old Bunny that was lost!" said the Boy. But he never knew that it really was his own Bunny, who had come back to look at the child who had helped make him Real.